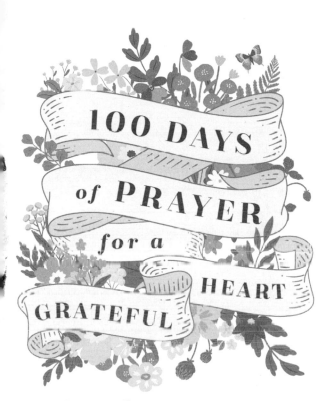

100 DAYS of PRAYER for a GRATEFUL HEART

Carolyn Larsen

Revell

a division of Baker Publishing Group
Grand Rapids, Michigan

© 2023 by Carolyn Larsen

Published by Revell
a division of Baker Publishing Group
Grand Rapids, Michigan
www.revellbooks.com

Printed in China

Library of Congress Cataloging-in-Publication Data
Names: Larsen, Carolyn, 1950– author.
Title: 100 days of prayer for a grateful heart / Carolyn Larsen.
Other titles: One hundred days of prayer for a grateful heart
Description: Grand Rapids, Michigan : Revell, a division of Baker Publishing Group, [2023] | Includes index.
Identifiers: LCCN 2022050888 | ISBN 9780800740849 (cloth) | ISBN 9781493443574 (ebook)
Subjects: LCSH: Prayers—Christianity.
Classification: LCC BV245 .L264 2023 | DDC 242/.8—dc23/eng/20230217
LC record available at https://lccn.loc.gov/2022050888

Baker Publishing Group publications use paper produced from sustainable forestry practices and post-consumer waste whenever possible.

23   24   25   26   27   28   29   7   6   5   4   3   2   1

Introduction

Dear gentle reader,

The freedom to actually talk to our heavenly Father is one of the greatest blessings of knowing him. Being able to share concerns that weigh on our hearts, asking for his guidance for decisions, and requesting his help with problems or his rescue or intervention in serious situations . . . all of these are wonderful privileges. It's possible that much of our prayer time is filled with these kinds of requests. We are grateful to bring them before our almighty, powerful, loving Father, and he is grateful to hear them. He even asks us to bring our concerns to him. He never intended for us to journey through life alone.

However, there is another type of prayer that can be too easily relegated to a smaller portion of our prayer time: the prayer of gratitude. It's so easy to get buried in the concerns and fears of the problems we face and forget to look around at the wonderful things God does for us every day.

I hope the prayers in this book will help remind you to simply be grateful for at least one thing each day. Working on these prayers has certainly been helpful for me.

One hundred prayers of gratitude are just the beginning of noticing the many, many blessings in our lives. And there's no doubt that an attitude of gratitude can go a long way in lifting sagging spirits. Prayers of gratitude help you turn the focus from what's going wrong to all that is good, grace-filled, and blessed. Your problems won't necessarily go away, but you will be reminded of God's work in your life and of his many blessings. Some of his blessings are seemingly small, everyday blessings, perhaps even ordinary. Some are big, absolutely miraculous works. All are evidence of his love.

Perhaps there is a specific point of gratitude filling your heart. If you would like some guidance on expressing your gratitude to the Lord, check out the index of topics at the back of this book. One of these prayers may help jump-start your conversation with God. As you read these prayers and allow the reminders of gratitude to sink into your heart, I pray that you will be encouraged to be truly thankful for all the good that is poured into your life each day. God's attention to detail is amazing. I pray that the awareness of his goodness will motivate you to look for ways to pour goodness into the lives of others. "Blessed so that you can also bless."

Blessings,
Carolyn

1

Morning Gratitude

Good morning, Father,

I woke to the pinkish light of dawn shining through my window. The promise of a new day. I'm grateful for the opportunities this day will bring. I already know it will offer me chances to choose to be kind or unkind to others. It will give my ego the opportunity either to leap forward or to take a step back so that I think of others before myself. I ask that you guide the words I say, the tone I use to speak, my actions, and even my facial expressions throughout this day. Father, help me be intentional in being kind and respectful. Keep in the forefront of my mind that I'm representing you in everything I do and each word I say.

Thank you that I woke with energy to help me start this day rested from a night of good sleep. Thank you that yesterday's shortcomings and failures belong to yesterday and that this is a new day. I'm excited for a fresh start. Oh God, I'm so grateful to have this day to serve you and those around me. Show me how to make the most of it from this early moment until I lay my head on the pillow again tonight. I give you this day, Lord, in gratitude and expectation!

The faithful love of the Lord never ends!
  His mercies never cease.
Great is his faithfulness;
  his mercies begin afresh each
    morning.

Lamentations 3:22–23

2

Cleansed
from Sin

My loving Father,

My heart is overflowing with thankfulness today. Some days, the honest realization of my unworthiness of your love, forgiveness, and grace just knocks me to my knees. I mean, it flattens me. I could be hopelessly broken by it, but your love picks me up. On these days . . . especially on these days . . . I'm amazed at your continuous forgiveness and grace.

Thank you, Father, for Jesus's sacrificial work on the cross. Thank you for your incredible love for me. Jesus's death and resurrection are the reasons my sins are forgiven. My sins are cast so far away that you don't even see them anymore. That amazes me! Oh God, I am so thankful that you look at me and see a clean heart, one that desires to serve and obey you even though I fail so often. I can't even find the words to express how thankful I am for your continual forgiveness, your amazing grace, and your love that knows no end. Thank you for Jesus, for the cross, for the empty tomb. Thank you that I can know you because of all Jesus has done.

You yourselves are a case study of what he does. At one time you all had your backs turned to God, thinking rebellious thoughts of him, giving him trouble every chance you got. But now, by giving himself completely at the Cross, actually dying for you, Christ brought you over to God's side and put your lives together, whole and holy in his presence.

Colossians 1:21–23 The Message

3

Constant Gratitude

Oh Father,

On the days that are hard, I try to be grateful for the lessons I'm learning. In the times when I'm lonely, I try to be thankful knowing you are always with me. On the days when I don't even like myself, I am so very grateful that not only do you like me, you love me . . . always. When so many situations or relationships seem totally hopeless, I'm grateful to remember that you know what's happening and you have a plan. In the times when I feel completely lost, I'm thankful for your clear and strong guidance. During the dark times when I'm confused, I'm grateful for your leadership. And oh God, there are the many, many times when I fail and am humbly grateful for your forgiveness and your second, third, and hundredth chances to do better. Even when thankfulness isn't on the top of my list, you forgive me and allow me time to reach a place of thankfulness again.

I have so very much to be thankful for each day. With every breath I take, there are new realizations of all you give me, teach me, and do for me. I don't always take time to notice those things. Or sometimes I am too caught up in . . . me. Eventually, my eyes and heart are opened, and I'm once again overwhelmed with gratefulness for your amazing love.

Praise the LORD.

Give thanks to the LORD, for he is good; his love endures forever.

Psalm 106:1 NIV

4

Thank You for Changing Hearts

Dear Father,

I am so very grateful that your love and power can change hearts. There are some people I simply give up on. I'm thinking of those who have committed the most horrific crimes against other humans, especially against children. When I hear those stories, my innate desire for justice wants to call down your angel armies on those people to make them pay for what they have done. And while they may pay on some level, eventually you remind me that you can change hearts. You can change people. After all, you changed me. I'm grateful that you look at people and see the possibilities that are there, under the sin. You see the potential. Of course, you see the sin and pain that sometimes make us behave the way we do, but you see more than that.

Thank you for opening our eyes and hearts to what we can be. Thank you for your patience and teaching as we learn and grow. Thank you for your deep, deep love. Thank you that no person is totally hopeless, because you don't give up, and your overwhelming, forgiving, grace-filled love is so very powerful. Thank you for changing my heart and for giving me the compassion to pray that you will do the same for others . . . even those I'm arrogantly tempted to deem hopeless.

This means that anyone who belongs to Christ has become a new person. The old life is gone; a new life has begun!

2 Corinthians 5:17

5

Praise for Creation

Dear Lord,

What fun you must have had thinking up the beautiful world you made for us. Thank you for sunshine and for the trees, plants, flowers, and bushes that our wonderful sun sustains. Thank you that a day filled with sunshine and a blue sky can nourish my own soul and lift my attitude high above troubling circumstances. Thank you for creating the massive oceans. I feel a great peace as I watch the waves methodically flow to shore, and that reminds me how steady and constant your love is. Creation is so much bigger than me. I often need to be re-minded of that. Thank you for gentle streams, for pastures with grasses blowing in the breeze. Thank you for snowcapped mountains.

Thank you for the incredible animals you made. God, you are so amazing. Giant whales. Tiny hummingbirds. Lions. Bears. Monkeys. Giraffes. Puppies. Kittens. So many different animals. Thank you for them.

Thank you for star-filled nights. Thank you for moonlight gently filling my room. Thank you for rain showers. Thank you for thunderstorms. Oh God, thank you for it all! Every blade of grass and grain of sand is a whisper of your love for us!

I just thank you for making things that all of us can appreciate and that can bring us to worship you. You thought of something for everyone!

Ah, Sovereign LORD, you have made the heavens and the earth by your great power and outstretched arm. Nothing is too hard for you.

Jeremiah 32:17 NIV

6

Thanks for
Kind Friends

Father,

Today I'm especially grateful for the correcting and challenging words that are gently spoken by friends and family and delivered with care and concern for me. Thank you for giving me people I trust because they have proven they have my best interests in mind. They challenge me to live out my love, honor, and respect for you so others can see the reality of how it changes me and impacts them.

Thank you that these loved ones consistently speak thoughtfully and with respect, challenging me with kind words, explaining any problems they have with the things they see me doing and saying—things that are disrespectful to you or unkind to others. The thing is that sometimes I don't even realize the impact of what I've said or done. Thank you for giving these dear ones the wisdom and respect to speak with me privately so I'm not embarrassed in front of others. Thank you for helping them choose their words carefully. I'm so grateful for their friendship and care. I pray that I may be as much of a blessing in their lives as they are in mine.

From a wise mind comes wise speech;
the words of the wise are persuasive.

Kind words are like honey—
sweet to the soul and healthy for the
body.

Proverbs 16:23–24

7

Gratitude for Making Me Me!

Father God,

I've spent way too much of my life comparing myself to others, feeling "less than" in so many areas, and dreaming of being better, mattering to others, or feeling more important. At times I've even convinced myself that I must be a disappointment to you.

Father, I want to thank you for opening my eyes to the out-and-out lies those thoughts have been. They started as one small chink in my self-confidence, and Satan wiggled his way in and kept hitting my self-esteem over and over until he had me doubting my worth to others and my worth to you.

Oh God, I am so thankful to know it's not necessary for me to work and work to change in order to pattern my life after someone else. Thank you that you made me just the way you want me, with the interests, talents, and gifts that make me who I am. Thank you that I can always learn to develop and strengthen the gifts you've given me—but I'm also fine just being me. I don't have to compare myself to anyone else. Thank you for relieving that pressure.

---

*You made all the delicate, inner parts of
    my body
and knit me together in my mother's
    womb.
Thank you for making me so wonderfully
    complex!
Your workmanship is marvelous—
    how well I know it.*

Psalm 139:13–14

8

Thankful for God's Amazing Love

My dear Father,

I am overwhelmed—no, actually, I'm completely blown away—by your amazing love. Thank you for loving me so well, so completely. You always know what I need much better than I do, even though I arrogantly argue with you once in a while. Because you are so wise, many times you don't give me what I ask for. I admit that sometimes that's hard to accept. But in hindsight, I always see that you answered by giving me what I needed and not what I wanted. You love me enough to teach me to trust you by saying no or not right now to some of my requests. You care enough for me to teach me patience through painful times of waiting, knowing that eventually I will recognize your true goodness and then learn to trust you a bit more completely. A step at a time.

Thank you for understanding when I react with unhappiness or frustration to not getting what I want. You understand why, and you continue to give me opportunities to learn . . . to believe that you always have my best interests in mind as you work out your plan in my life. Thank you for understanding that faith is a journey for us humans. It's a learning process. Thank you for your tender love. Thank you for your tough love. Thank you for your constant, amazing love.

Give thanks to the LORD, for he is good!
His faithful love endures forever.

1 Chronicles 16:34

9

The Blessing
of Salvation

Dear heavenly Father,

My heart is bursting with gratitude for the salvation you have made possible for me. I'm very aware that my salvation is only because of your sacrificial love. I know it cost you dearly. My salvation was not free for you, but it is for me. Thank you for loving me so much. Thank you for wanting to have a relationship with your creation.

I'm amazed yet so very thankful that Jesus was willing to come to earth from your perfect heaven because of his love for me . . . for all people. He came knowing what he would have to endure here. He knew people wouldn't listen to him, wouldn't trust him, would lie about him . . . would kill him to silence him even though he did nothing wrong. He only loved. He experienced unimaginable torture and three days of darkness and separation from you . . . for me. There are not enough words to express my gratitude. There is nothing I can give in response—except my heart. And I gladly give my heart and my life in thanks for your gift of salvation and the promise of eternity with you. Praise you for salvation bought by sacrifice.

For this is how God loved the world. He gave his one and only Son, so that everyone who believes in him will not perish but have eternal life. God sent his Son into the world not to judge the world, but to save the world through him.

John 3:16–17

10

God Sees My Heart

Dear heavenly Father,

It's painful to confess this, yet I know I must. Even though I see how much you do for me, and I know that you love me deeply . . . well, I don't always feel gratitude toward you. God, sometimes life is really hard. People are unkind. Situations are difficult and may even look pretty hopeless (at least from my perspective). There are times when I feel as though I'm living under a dark cloud and I can't find my way out. It's not easy to say thank you from under that dark cloud.

I'm so grateful for your patience with me in those dark times. Father, I can't even find the right words to thank you for seeing my heart and not just my attitude. I'm grateful that you know I honestly don't want to be like this. It's exhausting. I long to be so full of trust and hope that I can be truly, honestly thankful, even during hard times, even when I'm under a cloud—especially in those times. Thank you for staying close beside me when I'm struggling. I know that if I keep reaching out to you, looking for the big and small reminders of your presence, I'll get through the doubts and come out stronger on the other side. I'm so grateful that you stick with me.

Test me, LORD, and try me,
examine my heart and my mind;
for I have always been mindful of your
unfailing love
and have lived in reliance on your
faithfulness.

Psalm 26:2–3 NIV

11

True Gratitude for Good Health

Dear God,

Thank you for good health. I'm grateful that I am mobile enough to get out of bed every morning. I'm blessed to be well enough to do whatever work is before me each day—whether it's contributing at my job, cleaning my home, or working in the yard. I know there will be days when I won't be as active or have the energy to do everything, but I'm grateful for the energy to tackle the tasks of the day.

Thank you for a comfortable bed to rest in and for nutritious food that helps me stay healthy and gives me energy. Thank you for loved ones who encourage me, laugh with me, talk with me. Those things help me create and keep a positive attitude.

I have no doubt there will be some health struggles as I grow older. But Father, I'm grateful for every good day you give me. Help me enjoy my days and make the best of each one. Open my eyes to those who can't physically do the things I can do. Show me ways to help them and to do so with a joyful spirit, respecting their dignity. There are many people who do not have the blessing of good physical health or who are not granted a long life. May I never take these things lightly. I give you praise with gratitude for each breath I take.

Let all that I am praise the LORD;
may I never forget the good things he
does for me.
He forgives all my sins
and heals all my diseases.

Psalm 103:2–3

12

Praise for Who God Is

Oh God,

I confess that I'm sometimes tempted to give up—on myself, on others, on whole situations. I also confess that those times are when I'm depending on my own wisdom or strength instead of leaning on and listening to you. The frustrating thing is, I know I don't have to sink into this negativity. If I would just turn to you, recognize your mighty power, and ask for your help, things would be so much better. God, I celebrate right now that no other being—human or spirit—has the power to stand against you.

No argument, trickery, or sneakiness can fool you. Your wisdom knows no limits. You see all the future holds. Nothing blocks your sight, and nothing changes your plans. All your power and strength are constantly focused on me, and I see your love for me woven in them. Oh my loving Father, this truth should remind me always to turn to you first.

It's impossible to comprehend the magnitude of your love for me. Still, with what I can grasp, I praise you for your gentle love. I'm just one human among millions, yet you love me. I need only to let go and let you guide my life and direct my steps. And because of your power, strength, and love, I know I will always be exactly where I should be.

Yours, O Lord, is the greatness and the power and the glory and the victory and the majesty, for all that is in the heavens and in the earth is yours. Yours is the kingdom, O Lord, and you are exalted as head above all.

1 Chronicles 29:11 ESV

13

The Gift of Prayer

My loving Father,

Each and every day, I see evidence of your love in my life in an absolute multitude of ways. Moment to moment, it's clear how much you love me. I'm grateful for the many things you do for me and provide for me each day. I'm thankful for your guidance and support. Those are all wonderful things. But do you want to know what I'm most thankful for? This, right here . . . the gift of being able to talk to you. I'm grateful that you want to know what's on my heart, what worries me, what keeps me awake at night, whom I'm concerned about, who has pressing needs, what I need help with . . . you want to know it all! You have even *asked* me to talk with you.

I think the privilege you've given your children of praying is one of the greatest pieces of evidence of your love for us. It shows that you care about the day in and day out of our lives. It proves you're not just sitting up in heaven, directing our lives without caring about how we feel or what we're struggling with. You love us so much that you care about every detail. Thank you for prayer. Thank you for listening. Thank you for caring.

Don't worry about anything, but pray about everything. With thankful hearts offer up your prayers and requests to God.

Philippians 4:6 CEV

14

Your Amazing Grace

Father,

I've often heard *grace* defined as "God's riches at Christ's expense." I'll be honest: It's a challenge to even begin to understand that. Your riches are so magnificently, eternally unending, and the truth of Christ's sacrificial expense is difficult to comprehend. He gave his all for me . . . his place in heaven and then his very life. It's so hard to conceive his sacrifice, but the reality of it fills me with confidence in your love and grace.

When I mess up—okay, I'll say it—when I sin, you don't throw me into jail, get angry with me, or walk away from me in disgust. It's incredible, but you lovingly give me another chance, and then another and another, to grow and to learn how to be more like Jesus. As the old hymn says, your grace is amazing. It's hard to understand because we humans are seldom that forgiving and gracious to others. Your grace is a blessing and it is truly sufficient for me. It's really all I need. Thank you for your forgiving, loving grace.

He said to me, "My grace is sufficient for you, for my power is made perfect in weakness." Therefore I will boast all the more gladly about my weaknesses, so that Christ's power may rest on me.

2 Corinthians 12:9 NIV

15

Thank You for Your Protection

Oh Father,

I came very close to being in a terrible car accident today. Oh God, there were only inches between my vehicle and the other one. It was terrifying. I could see the other driver's face, and she was just as scared as I was. I sat in my car shaking for several minutes afterward. When I was finally able to take a deep breath, I thought about something incredible—I wonder how many times you've protected me. How many times have you saved me that I didn't even know about? How many times when I didn't even realize I was in danger? How often have you slowed me down (and I got frustrated because I would be late) to keep me from being hurt in an accident—or worse?

I would guess I've been oblivious to many, many times I could have been seriously hurt or worse, but you, in your loving-kindness, have protected me over and over. I know for a fact you have protected me from my own foolishness by not giving me what I've so boldly asked you for when I've been certain this thing, situation, or person would be good for me. I know you've kept me from hurting others by reining in my temper and shutting my mouth at just the right time. Thank you so much for your protection. It shows me how very much you love me.

You are my hiding place;
you will protect me from trouble
and surround me with songs of
deliverance.

Psalm 32:7 NIV

16

Grateful for My Struggles

Dear Lord,

I never thought I'd be able to honestly say this, but . . . thank you for hard times. I mean the times when the sky around me seems totally dark and I can't see any light at all; the times when the mountains before me are rugged and rocky and I don't have the strength to climb them; the times when I feel buried in quicksand that is sucking me farther and farther down; the times when I feel lost, defeated, and hopeless . . . thank you for those times. Oh Father, those struggles are so hard and so painful, but I know there are lessons I can learn as I trust you to get me through them.

I can say thank you because I've recently come to the point of honestly being grateful, even when I'm hurting, because you love me so much that you walk with me through the pain. You don't leave me alone in my hurt; you stay close beside me and teach me, strengthen me . . . love me. I know you're there, gently turning my thoughts to you and your Word. No experience, no struggle, nothing is wasted with you. I learn to lean on you. I learn to know your Word. Not just know it but trust it.

God is good,
  a hiding place in tough times.
He recognizes and welcomes
  anyone looking for help,
No matter how desperate the trouble.

Nahum 1:7 The Message

17

Thankful for Self-Forgiveness

Father,

I am grateful that you forgive my sins, but the truth is that I have a hard time forgiving myself for some things. I need your help to forgive myself. It isn't easy to do, partly because I feel terrible about the mistakes I've made. That's bad enough, but I feel even worse about the times I've been intentionally unkind or selfish and have hurt others. I confess these things to you and believe you forgive me. Then I try to forgive myself and even think I've done it, but in the darkness of night, the condemning thoughts come rushing back. Oh God, I'm very grateful that you don't condemn me for my failures. I know that when I confess my sins and ask your forgiveness, you give it freely and once and for all, and my sins are totally gone from your sight. It is all over and done with.

I'm grateful that when you look at me, you don't see my failures. You see your daughter who is yearning to be like Jesus and learning how to do that a step at a time. You see that my heart wants to learn and grow. Thank you that with you each and every day begins as a clean slate, not clouded by yesterday's sins and failures. Help me learn to forgive myself so that for me each day is a fresh start too.

If our hearts condemn us, we know that God is greater than our hearts, and he knows everything.

1 John 3:20 NIV

18

Thank You for Rain

Oh God,

It's raining . . . again. It's a dark, cold, damp day filled with constant downpours. The weather changed my plans for the day. I can't work in the yard. I don't want to go anywhere because I have no desire to be out in the rain. But here's the thing: I'm home alone and actually grateful for some downtime. I have a stack of books to read, and I just picked the one on top. I'll enjoy cups of warm tea while I snuggle under a blanket. Most importantly, I began this rainy day by spending time with you, reading Scripture and meditating on it.

To be honest, I don't take this much time with you when I've got a busy day of appointments, errands, or time spent with friends. So I want to thank you for the rain. It's good for the grass, flowers, and trees. It helps them grow. It's good for my growth too because I spent more time with you and felt the warmth of your presence. Then I relaxed as I read and napped a bit, and that's good for my soul too. Even though the rain changed my plans and interrupted my schedule, I am thankful for it—for its nourishment to the earth and for the rest it brought to my spirit

---

Come near to God, and he will come near to you.

James 4:8 CEV

19

Never Alone

Dear Father,

I like people. Especially my family and friends. I enjoy stimulating conversation. I love when we laugh together. I appreciate how we care for one another and share what's happening in each other's lives. Recently though, because of . . . well, life . . . many people have felt even more isolated and alone. Stressful things are happening in our world. Treasured friends and family move away. Changes in work situations mean seeing fewer people than before. This all adds up to more and more loneliness.

I'll admit that for a while I felt pretty sorry for myself, but lately I look around and see the proof that I am not alone . . . ever. You are with me every moment of the day. Thank you for the reminders of your presence that come in such simple ways: a cardinal perched on a branch outside my window, a favorite song of praise on the radio, a verse about your presence and love popping into my mind. I know none of those things are "accidents" and that they are lovely reminders from you. I am so grateful to have you going before me, guarding behind me, always present with me. Family and friends will float back in, and I'll enjoy them, but I am so blessedly grateful for your presence with me every minute of every day.

You hem me in behind and before,
and you lay your hand upon me.
Psalm 139:5 NIV

20

Gratitude for the Holy Spirit's Work

Father,

Today I am especially thankful that your Holy Spirit lives in my heart. What a wonderful gift his presence is. Scripture tells me that he guards my salvation. I am yours, Father, and your Spirit protects my position with you. No one can snatch me away from you. I'm so grateful for that.

I am often aware of your Holy Spirit's presence by his little nudges that seek to guide my behavior and decisions. Sometimes I say that I feel something "in my gut," but I know in reality those feelings and nudges come from him. He's like a little tap on my shoulder that says, "Do you really want to say that? . . . do that? . . . behave that way?" When I'm listening to him, I know that my behavior is more like Jesus's and that I am living in a way that shows Jesus is important to me. My life can show others who Jesus is and how he loves. Oh Father, I want to do that more and more. So, with a grateful heart for the Spirit's presence and guidance, I ask for the courage, strength, and wisdom to listen to him more consistently. Thank you for his presence and guidance and protection.

In him you also, when you heard the word of truth, the gospel of your salvation, and believed in him, were sealed with the promised Holy Spirit, who is the guarantee of our inheritance until we acquire possession of it, to the praise of his glory.

Ephesians 1:13–14 ESV

21

The Blessing
of Friends

Dear Father,

I want to thank you for my friends. Seriously, you knew just the right group of people to place in my life. There are some who make me laugh so hard I cry, and that sweet laughter refreshes my soul. Laughing so hard I can't catch my breath is just the medicine I need some days to lift my mood, change my focus, and increase my energy. Other friends engage me in deep, challenging conversations that make me think critically about my opinions and beliefs.

Still others push me to think deeper, think for myself, and challenge things I've just accepted as truth without researching them. They hold me accountable in my walk with you. And then there are the dear friends who seem to always know just the right thing to say. They even sit quietly with me when I'm hurting, knowing words aren't necessary. They bring coffee or soup. They love and care in the most practical ways.

Thank you for this group of friends so precious to me, so necessary to me. You know just whom I need at any given moment, and you send them to my door or to my phone. Thank you for loving me through them!

Two people are better off than one, for they can help each other succeed. If one person falls, the other can reach out and help. But someone who falls alone is in real trouble.

Ecclesiastes 4:9–10

22

Thank You
for Rest

Oh God,

It's been a long, stressful day. Challenges hit me that I never expected. They were complete surprises . . . and not good ones. I did my best to deal with each thing in a way that honored you and respected the people involved. Maybe I did a good job. Maybe I didn't. Either way, it has drained me of energy and hope. Frankly, I'm grateful this day is over. I'm grateful I can climb into my soft bed with warm blankets and close my eyes.

Thank you for rest, Father. I pray that you will prevent the stresses of this day from creeping into my thoughts and interrupting my rest. I ask you to fill my heart with your peace and the confidence that you will handle all situations and even clean up any messes I unintentionally made. I'm just spent, and I long for rest that can only come from you. So, thank you again for nighttime, for home, for quiet, for confidence in you. Thank you for rest to restore my mind, heart, and body so that I can face a new day tomorrow, refreshed and strengthened by rest.

God cares for you, so turn all your worries over to him.

1 Peter 5:7 CEV

23

Gratitude for Possibilities

Father,

Sometimes I feel like a benchwarmer. What I mean is that I feel like I'm on the sidelines watching others play the game. I want to get in the game, but secretly I'm not sure I can keep up with the big kids anyway. I quickly sink into the "poor me" mode of thinking that I missed the distribution of intellect, talent, or creativity. Dejected, I think you must be so disappointed in me.

But here's the thing: When I have those kinds of thoughts, you stop me. You actually stop me!

It feels like you put your hands on my cheeks and physically turn my eyes to look at the things you've helped me do. You show me the ways you've uniquely gifted me and how you've given me opportunities to use those gifts. I love that! You show me there are no limits for what I can do—except my own negativity. You see possibilities for me that are greater than I can begin to imagine. You want good things for me and actually plan good things for me. You won't let my inhibitions or poor self image hold me back. Thank you for believing in me. Thank you for making me just the way you want me to be.

Jesus replied, "What is impossible with man is possible with God."

Luke 18:27 NIV

24

Joy for Weekends

Oh Father,

What joy to wake up this morning without hearing the buzz of an annoying alarm clock. The relaxing pleasure of lingering in my warm bed for a while, thinking about the day ahead and how I might spend my time, thinking about you and thanking you for the wonderful blessing of weekends off work. Thank you for downtime. You know how important it is—you even took a day of rest when creating this world!

It's refreshing to give my mind a day free of work responsibility and stress. It's an opportunity to spend time with family and friends. And yes, there is time to get some chores done at home that there simply is not time for during the week. It's medicine for my soul that I can sit and read Scripture longer than I do on a work-day. It's relaxing and fulfilling, and your Word feeds me. Thank you, Father, for days of rest. I work hard all week to be a good employee and coworker. I take my responsibilities seriously. Thank you for weekend time to be with friends and family whom I enjoy and to do fun things together. Thank you for knowing how important rest would be.

Then Jesus said, "Come to me, all of you who are weary and carry heavy burdens, and I will give you rest."

Matthew 11:28

25

My Partnership with God

Dear God,

Do you want to know what totally blows my mind? I mean, it takes my breath away, and yet the responsibility of it kind of frightens me. I'm talking about the privilege of being a partner with you in your work on earth. Wow. What an honor. Thank you for trusting me. Thank you for wanting my service. Thank you for gifting me with interests, talents, and compassion you can use to draw others to you. It's a responsibility I do not take lightly.

I'm grateful to have a role in something so important. Thank you for giving me opportunities to create friendships that often lead to conversations about you. Thank you for giving me the right words to say when I have the opportunity to speak about you. Thank you for providing ways for me to serve others and show them your love by how I treat them, speak to them, and respect them. Thank you for reminding me to be careful of how I speak about others and not blurt out my opinions. Thank you for guiding my words as I speak about you so people aren't put off by what I say. Thank you that I can converse with people, even if I don't agree with the way they live their lives. I couldn't have a part in your work if I didn't have empathy for them. Oh God, it's such an unexpected, amazing honor and responsibility. Thank you so much!

So we are Christ's ambassadors; God is making his appeal through us. We speak for Christ when we plead, "Come back to God!"

2 Corinthians 5:20

26

The Gift of Encouragement

Father,

I want to thank you for the pats on the back and words of encouragement I received from some people today. I know I shouldn't require those kinds of things, and I don't really, but you know once in a while those things are so nice to hear.

I enjoy volunteering in a few ministries and organizations. Of course, I don't do it to get recognition. But sometimes I do get tired. I get discouraged. I question whether anything I'm doing really matters to anyone. However, in your wisdom and by your grace, you always send someone who unexpectedly thanks me for something I've done. Now and then, it's a person I don't even know who says she appreciates an act of service or a kind word and smile I've offered. That's special. It's always a surprise. Thanks, too, for the friends and coworkers who take the time to say, "Good job." Their kind words of appreciation motivate me to keep on serving, keep on working, keep on smiling and being friendly. Thank you for knowing when I need a little encouragement to get me over the hump of discouragement. It's a privilege to serve others, and it's nice to be thanked.

Therefore encourage one another and build each other up, just as in fact you are doing.

1 Thessalonians 5:11 NIV

27

Thankful for a Day of Worship

Dear Father,

Whew. What a week it's been. The chaos has been growing every day. I am so very grateful that you instruct us to set aside a day in our week to gather with other Christians to praise and worship you. It's a real breath of fresh air after a crazy week. I'm grateful for the community that our joint worship time creates. Thank you for my church and for the instruction I receive there from your Word. Thank you for the times of corporate prayer we share. The times we pray together for one another and for things happening in our world are truly precious, and I know that our joined heart requests rise to you. I appreciate that we can lift our voices together in sweet praise to you. The sound of all those voices praising you encourages my heart and must sound wonderful to you! I'm grateful, too, for the work we can do in our own community to help others and for the kingdom work we support around the world so that others may learn about you.

Of course, I try to thank and praise you each day on my own, but some days I get lost in the struggle of problems. That's one reason having a day of worship set aside in my week means so much to me.

Praise God in his holy house of worship,
  praise him under the open skies;
Praise him for his acts of power,
  praise him for his magnificent
    greatness.

Psalm 150:1–2 The Message

28

Thankful for Safe Water

Father,

I know that I take much for granted in this blessed city where I live. One thing I don't really even think about is that I can have a drink of cold, refreshing water anytime I want. There are so many people in this world who are not able to do that. Many have to take a long trek to draw water from a river or lake. Their water isn't purified or safe like mine is.

Thank you, Lord, for safe, purified drinking water. I don't have to be concerned that my glass of water will make me sick. I'm not worried that there won't be enough water today or tomorrow or the next day. It's amazing that where I live, there is water to irrigate crops and to water our lawns. We have water for swimming pools and water parks. We have more than enough. Yet so many people in other places do not even have enough to drink. Father, in my deep gratitude for the blessing of clean water, show me ways to contribute to organizations that are trying to provide water in other countries. Open my eyes and heart to specific needs and ways to help.

This same God who takes care of me will supply all your needs from his glorious riches, which have been given to us in Christ Jesus.

Philippians 4:19

29

God's Plan for Me

Oh God,

I'm grateful that you have a plan for my life—a good plan, a perfect plan. I know that what you desire for me is better than anything I plan for myself. Oh sure, I arrogantly make my plans and then pray for you to endorse them. You don't always do that though. Sometimes I'm disappointed or upset with you, but always, always, always, it becomes apparent that your plan is better than mine. I see that while I'm foolishly willing to settle for coal, you generously want to give me diamonds.

I'm so glad you see into the future. You know what tomorrow holds and the next day and the next. You see how all the pieces fit together. You know what I'm capable of much better than I do. Thank you that when a door closes or you don't answer my requests the way I hope you will, it's only because something better, grander, more satisfying is ahead for me. Thank you for not letting me settle for less. Thank you for believing in me, trusting me to obey, and equipping me for what is ahead.

With all your heart
you must trust the LORD
    and not your own judgment.
Always let him lead you,
and he will clear the road
    for you to follow.

Proverbs 3:5–6 CEV

30

The Gift of Laughter

Oh Lord,

It's been a tough few days due to crises at work, some difficult relationships, an unexpected expense, terrible occurrences around the world . . . whew. Heavy things. Sometimes I feel like bad stuff is piling up, one on top of the other. But tonight when I sat down to read a new book, I was barely a page into it when I giggled. What an unexpected joy. The more I read, the more I smiled, giggled, then actually laughed out loud. What a stress buster laughter is! I felt so much better after a hearty laugh, even though nothing had changed in any area of my life.

Thank you for laughter, whether it comes from a conversation with a friend, through a TV program, from a book, or just from a delightful memory. Thank you that the hormones released by laughter serve to brighten my mood and improve my outlook on life. Sometimes I have to be willing to laugh—to let the humor cut through sorrow, depression, or a bad attitude. When I allow that, I always feel better. Laughter also improves my health, not just my attitude! You knit my body so perfectly that laughter can overpower any negativity I'm holding. Thank you for that!

A cheerful disposition is good for your health;
gloom and doom leave you bone-tired.

Proverbs 17:22 *The Message*

31

Grateful My God Is Near

My loving Father,

My heart is broken. I am inconsolable. Losing someone so dear to me has simply wrecked me. Father, this loss makes me more thankful than ever that you are here with me. I am so grateful that you are not a faraway God who sits up high in his heaven and doesn't see or pay attention to my pain and grief. You actually care. You care more than I can begin to imagine. You don't turn away from my pain; you actually come closer to comfort my broken heart.

Thank you for understanding the loss I feel. Thank you for caring that I hurt. And oh Father, how I hurt! I know you're near because even as tears roll down my cheeks, I have a peace deep in my heart knowing that you are in control and that you care. A peace that could only come from you. This loss did not take you by surprise. This peace gives me the knowledge that I'm loved. Even though you aren't here physically, like a human, your Spirit is in my heart, caring, loving, and encouraging. I'm so grateful that he brings Scriptures of comfort to my mind. I appreciate the worship songs of comfort that he hums to my heart. Oh God, thank you for being close beside me in my darkest times.

Even when I walk
*   through the darkest valley,*
I will not be afraid,
*   for you are close beside me.*
Your rod and your staff
*   protect and comfort me.*

Psalm 23:4

32

Thank God for Interruptions

Dear God,

Sometimes you open my eyes to new lessons in Bible passages I've read many times before. For example, I had an epiphany about how many times during Jesus's work he was on his way to this place or that place when his journey was interrupted . . . and that's when a miracle took place. A sick woman was cured, a dead girl was brought back to life, a leper was healed . . . so many times the real story was in the interruption, not in what his plans had been.

So, I want to be grateful for interruptions in my life. I'm often too quick to complain about them because they disturb my plans. But Father, when I think about it, those interruptions often lead to good conversations or to caring for a friend who's hurting. Sometimes it's a moment of laughter with someone that slows me down and makes me change direction. Thank you for reminding me that Jesus handled interruptions with grace and purpose because he knew that you are in control of every moment of our lives. He knew that interruptions are orchestrated by you to put us in the place we need to be in at any given moment in order to serve, care for, and help someone who needs us.

Thank you, God, for being in control of every moment. The next time I face an interruption, help me look for the interruption miracle in it, which is the blessing of serving you.

We can make our plans,
  but the LORD determines our steps.

Proverbs 16:9

33

Thankful
for the Bible

My generous Father,

Thank you for the Bible, your Word to me. Some days it reads like a love letter from you assuring me of your gentle care. Other times, the words that stand out are ones of power and strength, telling that you can get me through any crisis or challenge. I love the stories that show me how you cared for your people, guiding them, protecting them, and teaching them. The Bible itself tells me that its words are for my instruction so that I may get to know you better and learn to live in obedience and service.

Thank you for recording the stories of Jesus's life and ministry. I'm grateful to read how he loved people . . . even those thought by others to be unlovable. It's through seeing Jesus caring for others that I can learn to show care and love to others. I also thank you that Scripture itself tells us that you inspired its words. It has the messages in it that you want us to learn and remember. I am so very grateful for your Word and how it impacts my life. I love spending time reading and learning from it.

By your words I can see where I'm going;
they throw a beam of light on my
dark path.
I've committed myself and I'll never turn
back
from living by your righteous order.

Psalm 119:105 The Message

34

A Giving Heart

Father,

Thank you for giving me the sensitivity to notice when a gift might be an encouragement to someone. Sometimes a gift might be time spent chatting over a cup of coffee. Other times it could be picking up groceries or driving someone to a doctor's appointment. Once in a while it could be gifting someone a book or a meal out.

I pray that you'll guide me to generously give to others. Help me choose who might need a bit of encouragement from a small gift of time, energy, or money. Help me enjoy the fun of giving without expecting anything in return. When I get the opportunity, give me the right words to speak to give you all the credit for making gifts a possibility. I pray that my generosity might be evidence of your love to all who receive the gifts.

Give, and you will receive. Your gift will return to you in full—pressed down, shaken together to make room for more, running over, and poured into your lap. The amount you give will determine the amount you get back.

Luke 6:38

35

The Gift of Faith

Father,

I don't take the gift of faith lightly. I celebrate it because it means I believe that Jesus is your Son and that he came to earth to teach about you. He was persecuted, though he did nothing wrong. He was crucified to pay the penalty for *my* sins. But you raised him back to life, and he is alive.

Your Spirit lives in my heart to guide my walk with you. He teaches, challenges, and corrects me. I am absolutely certain that I will be with you for eternity. I am saved from my sins and the condemnation of being separated from you forever. I can believe all of this because of . . . faith. It hasn't always come easily to me. In fact, some say that I "fight my way to faith." But that's okay because you know my heart, and you see that when I fight through doubts and questions, my faith grows even stronger and more personal.

Thank you for faith. Thank you for teaching me through the doubts and questions. Thank you for experiences that strain and then strengthen my faith muscles. I am so very grateful.

This Good News tells us how God makes us right in his sight. This is accomplished from start to finish by faith. As the Scriptures say, "It is through faith that a righteous person has life."

Romans 1:17

36

Thank You for Your Joy

Oh Jesus,

Joy is flooding my heart. Real, honest-to-goodness joy. Thank you that the promise of your presence can make me joyous even in the most difficult times. Thank you that joy in my heart does *not* mean that I'm always smiling, laughing, or singing. Being happy does not mean being joyous. Being sad doesn't mean I don't have joy. That's because joy is deeper than happiness. It comes from the assurance of your presence in my heart, and oh Father, I am always certain of your presence. Joy is a gift that comes from knowing I am never alone to face whatever comes my way. You have promised to be with me always. Joy comes from knowing, believing, and trusting that you are strong and powerful and that no other being or power can stand against you. You have my back, and I trust you to get me through any circumstance I face. Joy means I know I am eternally, forever, moment-by-moment yours, and nothing and no one can pull me away from you.

Thank you for the certainty that joy brings—so much deeper and more real than the fleeting moments of happiness. I certainly enjoy being happy—I don't mean to diminish that—but my faith, my future, my certainty rest on joy!

You make known to me the path of life;
in your presence there is fullness of joy;
at your right hand are pleasures
forevermore.

Psalm 16:11 ESV

37

Thankfulness Always

Father,

Most of the time I remember to thank you when things are going well. Okay, I admit the thanks usually come after I've enjoyed things for a while. Eventually I do remember to be grateful; it's just not always right up front.

But, what I'm *not* good at is honestly and sincerely being thankful when things aren't going well . . . those times when life is tough and it seems like you aren't doing anything to make it easier. I don't gladly thank you for the hard times. That's not fair though, is it? I'm willing to take the good that you give me but not the difficult you allow.

Help me, Father, to be thankful for all things at all times. Help me to stop complaining and to stop wanting to have more, to have easier, to have . . . well, whatever I want. Help me to be thankful for lessons learned through struggle, for strength gained through persistence, for faith grown through trust, for peace found in life's storms. A shallow kind of faith won't grow a truly thankful heart, so Father, thank you for the painful, stretching, confusing times. Thank you for teaching me through them. Thank you for the reminders that you know how hard things are. You know how I hurt. You never, not even for one moment, leave me alone. Thank you.

Be cheerful no matter what; pray all the time; thank God no matter what happens. This is the way God wants you who belong to Christ Jesus to live.

1 Thessalonians 5:16–18 The Message

38

The Power of Forgiveness

Father,

I confess that I'm not very good at forgiving others. When someone offends me or hurts me, I'm a champion at feeling hurt, pouting, and holding a grudge. Whew. I realized recently how very wrong those feelings are and also how very unfair. Your examples of love, grace, and forgiveness are eye-opening and convicting. Thank you for forgiving my thoughts, words, attitudes, and behaviors many, many times each day. Thank you for not only forgiving but forgetting—pushing my sins "as far as the east is from the west" (Ps. 103:12 NIV). You don't hold a grudge. You don't punish. You don't pout. You simply forgive each time I ask (and possibly even when I don't).

The depth of your love and grace is mind-blowing. Your willingness to forgive over and over . . . often for the same repeated, self-centered sins . . . shows me how very much you love me and want a deep, intimate relationship with me. I'm so very grateful. So undeserving, but so very, very grateful.

With that example in the forefront of my mind, I will strive to do better at forgiving others. That will free my own heart from the constraints of grudge holding. Thank you for your forgiveness and for helping me with mine.

Stop being bitter and angry and mad at others. Don't yell at one another or curse each other or ever be rude. Instead, be kind and merciful, and forgive others, just as God forgave you because of Christ.

Ephesians 4:31–32 CEV

39

God Never Changes

Dear Father,

It feels like our world is on double fast-forward these days. There are so many changes, I simply can't keep up. I wonder sometimes if it's all actually progress. As I work through these things—learning technology so I can maneuver in our culture, understanding how relationships have changed in a virus-impacted world, recognizing the way social media has made our world bigger in some ways yet smaller in others—there is one huge thing I'm so very thankful for, and that is the truth that *you*, my loving Father, never change.

Scripture tells me you are the same yesterday, today, and tomorrow. What I read about your character in Scripture is as true today as it was two thousand years ago and will be two thousand years in the future. You were, are, and will be trustworthy and loving. You insist on my worship of you alone and my obedience to your Word because you know that obedience will mean a good life for me. Father, I'm grateful for your consistency. I'm thankful to know that in this fast-changing world, you will always be exactly who you've declared yourself to be. I can depend on that!

Jesus Christ is the same yesterday, today, and forever.

Hebrews 13:8

40

Thankful You Are My Waymaker

My Father,

Sometimes I lose my way. Sometimes I take the wrong path. I am grateful to know that you are my Waymaker, especially in the times when I feel lost in a deep fog. Those times are scary when I don't know what's ahead or can't see where to turn. Stepping into the darkness when I don't even know if there is solid footing ahead is terrifying. I know I can't go back in time, and standing still doesn't happen because life is always changing.

Father, your guidance is a blessing in every part of my life. From deciding on career choices, where to live, or ministry opportunities, to knowing when to work on relationships or walk away, I'm thankful that I don't have to make the big or the small decisions on my own. Thank you that you open doors and you close doors, and that tells me what you want me to do. I trust that your guidance will always lead me to the best place for me to grow as a person and to be useful in your kingdom work. Thank you for guiding my thoughts, my words, my decisions, and my actual steps.

The LORD says, "I will guide you along the best pathway for your life.
I will advise you and watch over you."

Psalm 32:8

41

Thankful for Wonderful Hope

Dear Father,

I don't know how people make it through this life without knowing you. What do they hold on to? How do they have any hope of the future being better? Everything is all on their own shoulders. That would terrify me! I'm thankful that I can be secure in your love, which means I can know without a doubt that my hope of eternity with you is secure. Thank you for that.

Your love promises me forgiveness for every rebellious, self-centered thought I have, every angry, judgmental word I speak. That's such a precious certainty of hope. My hope in you isn't a "maybe it's true" kind of hope; it's an absolute certainty. Thank you that I know beyond a shadow of a doubt that you love me and that your forgiveness is complete and constant. I know your Spirit lives in my heart, guiding and challenging me. My eternity with you in heaven is secure because of Jesus's sacrifice for my sins. My hope is in you. My hope is secure because of you. I am grateful for hope.

Now faith is the assurance of things hoped for, the conviction of things not seen.

Hebrews 11:1 ESV

42

Thank You for Your Wisdom

Dear Father,

I readily admit that my track record in making good decisions is not the best. I guess I make decisions and choices too quickly without having all the information I need. I admit that I can be pretty selfish and self-serving. These are all reasons I'm grateful for the wisdom you give in guiding me in my decision-making. Thank you for slowing me down sometimes so that I think a little deeper about the implications of my choices. Thank you for your Spirit in my heart that nudges me in a better direction than I'm heading. Thank you that I'm learning to pay attention to the little whispers of doubt that I know come from you when I'm about to make choices that will not be good for me or anyone else involved.

Thank you that when I forge ahead in my own stubborn will, you come along, clean up the mess I've made, and set me on a better path once again. I'm very grateful for your patient rescues. Thank you that your wisdom is available to me if I just ask and then wait for your guidance. I really cling to that.

If you need wisdom, ask our generous God, and he will give it to you. He will not rebuke you for asking.

James 1:5

43

Your Love for My Friend

Dear Father,

I'm really worried about a friend who is going through a pretty tough time right now. Okay, I know I have control issues, but I really think she's made some choices that are only making her situation harder. So far, I've managed to keep my opinions to myself (thanks for your help with that). I do love her, and it gives me great comfort to realize that you love her even more than I do. You see what's happening and you know the reasons behind all her actions.

Thank you for loving her. Thank you for staying close beside her. Thank you that you will continually work in her heart, reminding her of your love and care. Thank you that your strength and guidance are always available to her. Thank you that I can continue to lift her name to you, asking you to help her and care for her.

One more thing . . . please give me peace about this. I know that praying for her is the best thing I can do. You'll take care of her.

God remembered us when we were
down,
His love never quits.
Rescued us from the trampling boot,
His love never quits.
Takes care of everyone in time of need.
His love never quits.
Thank God, who did it all!
His love never quits!

Psalm 136:23–26 The Message

44

Thanks for Anger Lessons

Oh God,

Help me! I am so angry. I just want to throw a temper tantrum or hurt someone. I know I shouldn't feel that way, but . . . I'm being honest here . . . I want to make someone pay.

That was my prayer a few days ago. But Father, you've opened my eyes to a few things about my anger. Thank you for helping me see that while my anger sometimes flows from a sense of justice for myself or others, it can also come from a negative place. Sometimes my anger is because my selfish heart didn't get what it wanted. Sometimes I'm angry because someone dared to disagree with me. A self-centered, narcissistic attitude gets angry when it doesn't get its way. Relationships are damaged in the heat of anger. Words are spewed that leave scars on others' hearts. Anger doesn't change anyone's mind and seldom changes behaviors. Anger does no good.

Thank you for helping me learn about my anger. I don't like the self-focused attitude or behavior that causes my anger. I confess it to you and ask for your help in controlling it.

Understand this, my dear brothers and sisters: You must all be quick to listen, slow to speak, and slow to get angry. Human anger does not produce the righteousness God desires.

James 1:19–20

45

Gratitude for Wisdom of Older Believers

Dear Lord,

I am honored to count among my friends a few people who are decades older than I am. What a beautiful blessing they are to me. I want to thank you that these dear men and women spend time talking with me, sharing memories of their lives and of things that have happened in our world. Thank you for the wisdom they share about life, careers, priorities, and relationships. These dear friends encourage me to consider what's really important in life, and they especially share wisdom about living for you.

The history these mature believers have with you is a treasure trove of wisdom and blessings. Thank you for all you've taught them and for how you are teaching me through their shared experiences. Help me pay attention to and learn from the wisdom they've gained through living life. Help me be a blessing to them by spending time with them, encouraging them, listening to their stories, and helping them in any way I can. Bless these dear ones in their golden years, Father, and give them many, many more years on this earth. I love them, and I am so very thankful for them.

Gray hair is a glorious crown
worn by those
*   who have lived right.*
                    Proverbs 16:31 CEV

46

Thankfulness When I Feel Discouraged

Dear Lord,

Some days I feel so discouraged that I can barely hold my head up. I begin to think that everything and everyone is out to get me. I can't get away from the discouragement. I can't find peace. I can't find the proverbial light at the end of the tunnel. I try to be strong. I try to keep a good attitude, but it's hard, and I'm not very good at fighting off the discouragement.

Lord, I'm grateful that I don't have to deal with these negative feelings alone. I'm so very grateful that you are with me . . . right beside me every moment of every day. I know you will help me when I cry out to you. You will protect me, even from myself. You will lift me from the pit of anguish I have sunk myself into. You know why people are attacking me—or why it seems to me that they are. You will surround me with a shield of protection if I turn to you. I am thankful for you, Lord. I couldn't make it through these hard times without you. Lord, you are my Savior . . . every day.

You, Lord, are a shield around me,
my glory, the One who lifts my head
high.
I call out to the Lord,
and he answers me from his holy
mountain.

Psalm 3:3–4 NIV

47

Freedom to Worship

Father,

Thank you for opening my eyes to the fact that there's something I've taken for granted for a long time. I'm sad to confess that way too often I am lackadaisical about the freedom I have to worship you, to attend the church of my choice, to pray wherever I choose, and to share my faith openly. I'm grateful to live in a place where all of this is possible. I recognize that there are people in other places of the world who do not enjoy these freedoms.

I confess that I've become so used to being able to do all these things that I barely even think about them. Sometimes I feel like it's no big deal if I skip church for a week or two or if I put off prayer time until something "big" happens. And I'm sorry to admit that I seldom verbally share my faith. I'm sorry, Father. I really am. I am grateful for the opportunity to gather with other believers and worship you without fear that we will get in trouble. Thank you for the freedom to attend a church, to pray, and to tell others about your love. Oh Father, may I never take these freedoms lightly again!

Come, let us bow down in worship,
let us kneel before the Lord our
Maker.

Psalm 95:6 NIV

48

My God
of Miracles

Oh God,

I am thankful that you are not a God of average—that nothing at all is beyond your power. I'm thankful that the situations and the people I bring before you in prayer are not beyond your power and strength to handle, so I never need to feel hopeless. Thank you that you are the God of miracles—both big and small. Thank you that you hear my prayers and care about the things weighing on my heart. Thank you that you lovingly and generously give "everyday" miracles, like the sun rising, flowers blooming, a bed to sleep in, sufficient food to eat, and of course, a million other things you give every single day. Thank you that you give "big" miracles of health or healing, travel safety, restored relationships, loving families, and the blessing of friendships.

You are so good, Father. So good. Thank you for all you do for me and give me—miracles big and small!

O God! Your way is holy!
  No god is great like God!
You're the God who makes things
      happen;
  you showed everyone what you can do—
You pulled your people out of the worst
      kind of trouble,
  rescued the children of Jacob and
      Joseph.

                    Psalm 77:13–15 The Message

49

Grateful for the Promise of Heaven

Father,

My heart is broken. I lost a loved one today to a horrible, debilitating, mean disease. Oh Father, why don't you just stop these diseases that steal the personality, mind, and memories of people? Father, it's so painful to lose someone a day at a time and a memory at a time and for the possibility of any recognition to slowly disappear. It hurts. And now, after this slow, agonizing departure, she's gone. Really gone.

Even in my grief, though, there is one thing I am so very, very thankful for . . . well, two things really: One is that this dear one is out of pain. She no longer lives in that fearful fog of not knowing where she is or who people are. Her eyes were closed here, and when she opened them again, she was with you! I am thankful for that. And the other is that I am grateful that I will see her again. The promise of eternity with you rings truer than ever today. We both know you. We know that we will be reunited in your heaven one day. She'll be waiting for me, and we'll have eternity to laugh, talk, and enjoy our relationship. And praise you, Father, she will know who I am!

While we live in these earthly bodies, we groan and sigh, but it's not that we want to die and get rid of these bodies that clothe us. Rather, we want to put on our new bodies so that these dying bodies will be swallowed up by life.

2 Corinthians 5:4

50

Thankful for the Holy Spirit, Who Prays for Me

Father,

Sometimes I'm confused and conflicted, and I simply don't know how to pray for a situation or a person. I don't want to impose my personal will on the situation or the person's life. Even though I have an opinion as to what is best for everyone involved, I know my will may not be your will. Times like these are when I'm so very thankful that the Holy Spirit will pray for the things I can't find the right words to pray for. Thank you for your promise that he will do that for me. He will step into the gap and cover people and things in prayer when I just can't find the strength or the words to pray. The presence of the Holy Spirit in my life is such a gift. He does so much for me, and having my back in prayer is just one of those things. Thank you, Father, especially for this act by your Spirit. You know how important I believe prayer to be, and when I can't pray or don't know how to pray, I find great comfort in knowing . . . believing . . . that the Spirit is handling things for me. Thank you for that.

The Holy Spirit helps us in our weakness. For example, we don't know what God wants us to pray for. But the Holy Spirit prays for us with groanings that cannot be expressed in words.

Romans 8:26

51

Thankful for My Job

Dear Lord,

I am thankful that I have a job that I enjoy and coworkers who make it even more pleasant. I'm grateful for my manager, who is fair and kind and who treats me and the other employees with respect. I'm really grateful that I earn enough money to meet my needs—not always my wants but certainly my needs. Father, you always provide what I need and sometimes even a little extra. Maybe I didn't end up in the career I planned, but where I landed has turned out well. I'm grateful I have a job. So many others do not, or at least not one that meets their financial needs.

Thank you for directing my steps to this point. I look back over the years and see your hand as you moved me from job to job and company to company. You knew what I'd need to learn in each place in order to prepare me for the next step. Thank you for guiding me to this point. I'm excited to see what the future holds —whether I stay in this job or you have something else for me.

The LORD directs the steps of the godly. He delights in every detail of their lives.

Psalm 37:23

52

Thankful
for Choices

Father,

I'm grateful that you chose to give humans the
freedom to make our own choices. Do I always
make good ones? No. I know that you will direct
my choices if I ask you to and if I am willing to
pay attention to your direction, but you are not
pushy or demanding.

Thank you for helping me learn by allowing
me to stumble. It hurts sometimes. I wonder if
it hurts you too. But you let me make my own
choices, from choosing to believe that Jesus is

who he says he is and then asking him to be my Savior, to making daily choices about my own life. Sometimes I mess up royally, but thankfully you don't give up on me. You get me back on track, and that shows me just how much you love me. Sometimes I am grandly rebellious, but you don't walk away. You wait quietly for me to get my thoughts straight again and come back to you. Thank you for showing me how much you love me by letting me make choices, fall, and get up again. I learn from each decision I make that your way is always going to be the best for me.

"I know the plans I have for you," says the LORD. "They are plans for good and not for disaster, to give you a future and a hope.

Jeremiah 29:11

53

The Gift of Friendship

Dear Lord,

It is always a blessing to spend time with a friend, even if it was just over a quick cup of coffee. I know it may not have seemed like a big deal . . . but it was. It made me so happy to sit with another woman who "gets me." We understand each other so well and we often have deep, heartfelt conversations. What a gift that is. I can be totally honest with this friend and know that I will not face criticism or judgment. She gives only concern and love.

Thank you, Father, for this friend who honestly wants to know how I'm doing. She truly cares about what's going on in my heart and my life. Thank you for giving me a friend who has such wisdom and insight. She challenges me in my spiritual walk and encourages me to stay close to you. Thank you that she lives her faith out loud. She's an inspiration to me to do the same. I care about her life, family, and faith, along with the challenges she faces, just as she cares about mine. Our friendship is reciprocal. So, today's coffee time wasn't really about the coffee. It was about connecting with my friend, sharing life, sharing stories, and sharing love. Thank you, Father, for such a special friend.

Let us think of ways to motivate one another to acts of love and good works.

Hebrews 10:24

54

Thankful
I'm Still Here

Father,

What a privilege it is to be this old. Seriously, I've already lived longer than my parents did. I've even outlived my younger brother, my only sibling. I never expected to live to this age, and it feels kind of strange. It's an honor though. Thank you for keeping me in this life. You must have a purpose for me or I wouldn't still be here. I've had friends who would be the same age I am, but they have already gone to heaven. I don't take lightly the privilege of aging, seeing my children and grandchildren grow up, and being a part of their lives.

Oh sure, there are aches and pains and limitations with the aging of my physical body, but there are lessons and blessings to my spirit beyond compare as I learn more about living for you. So, thank you that I'm still here. Thank you for purpose in my life. Thank you that I can share wisdom with younger women from what I've learned. Of course, I look forward to being with you in heaven someday and to reuniting with loved ones who are already there. But for now, thank you for my life and age, and let's keep going!

I will be your God throughout your lifetime—
until your hair is white with age.
I made you, and I will care for you.
I will carry you along and save you.

Isaiah 46:4

55

Gratitude for (and to) Those Who Serve

Father,

I am blown away by the sacrifices of people who will put their lives on hold to go all over the earth to help others. These are people who leave their families, their jobs, their comforts to travel to places where natural disasters have hit or where people are in terrible poverty. They give of themselves to serve others. They provide food and water and even show people how to take care of their own needs until their city or province gets back on its feet. They treat people with dignity and respect and ask nothing in return. Without preaching a sermon, they are your compassion, your hands and feet, in a time of need.

Thank you, Father, for these generous, loving people who go and serve, often spending their own money. They love as you say your people should love by laying down their lives, giving their time and energy. Oh God, I am blessed to know about these people. I want very much to serve as they do—sacrificially.

Whoever would save his life will lose it, but whoever loses his life for my sake will save it.

Luke 9:24 ESV

56

Thank You for Protecting My Grandchildren

Father,

Thank you that my grandchildren came home safely from school today. Some children didn't. Thank you that thus far there hasn't been a threat in their school, even though they have to do drills for how to react if there is a problem. (I'm sad that they have to do these drills yet grateful that they do them.) I feel a bit guilty thanking you for their safety when there are moms, dads, and grandparents who can't say their children came home safely today too. My heart aches for them. It really does. I don't know the answer to this madness, God, but you do.

Oh God, my heart is divided between sorrow for those who have lost children and gratitude that it wasn't us . . . this time. My heart is filled with gratitude for your protection and yet sorrow for those who are hurting. Comfort them. Surround them with your love. Give them peace. Oh God, give them peace.

The Lord is faithful, and he will strengthen you and protect you from the evil one.

2 Thessalonians 3:3 NIV

57

God's Constant Faithfulness

Father,

I've been thinking about how to describe what your faithfulness means to me. I'm grateful for your faithfulness, but how do I explain it to someone who doesn't know you? What does it look like and feel like? As I think about it, I guess I'd say that your faithfulness shows me your committed loyalty to me. That means that you never give up on me. You don't leave me when I sin. You believe I can grow and learn and do better. Your faithfulness means you are constantly with me, loving me and forgiving me. You never waver. Your faithfulness to me is always there. What a comfort that is. The Bible tells me you go before me, you follow behind me—I am surrounded by you, and nothing can change that (Ps. 139:5). Your faithfulness means you are always present to guide me, teach me, and protect me. Always. Every minute of every day.

Thank you for your faithfulness to me. It is evidence of your steady, never-changing, faithful love.

If we are not faithful,
  he will still be faithful.
Christ cannot deny
  who he is.
    2 Timothy 2:13 CEV

58

Your Endless Supply of Strength

Oh Father,

Thank you for infusing my heart with your amazing strength at just the times when I most need superhuman power. I love to read the stories in the Bible of how you strengthened your people as they obeyed you and followed you. Those stories encourage me, but then, sadly, I go about my life not really thinking about your strength very much. I know, though, that it's like a secret weapon that's stashed below the surface, hidden away until I do need it, then *boom*, there it is. Thank you that every time I sink into a place of fearfulness or become paralyzed by worry, I can turn to you, and your strength floods into my heart. It lifts me out of negative thoughts and sets my focus on you. When I am depending on you, I know that nothing can defeat me, because your strength makes me powerful. Thank you for empowering me to face any obstacle, any problem, any foe. With you, I can do anything!

I can do everything through Christ, who gives me strength.

Philippians 4:13

59

Grateful That I Need to Please Only God

My Father,

People can be mean, judgmental, and critical. They say hurtful things right to my face or sometimes behind my back or through social media. Some try so very hard to make me fit their image of who I should be, and that's often a mirror of who they are.

Thank you for the realization that I don't need to become who they think I should be.

I'm grateful that your opinion of me is the only one that matters. Father, thank you that you made me with the personality and character you wanted me to have. Thank you that I don't need to conform to someone else's ideas. However, help me be kind and respectful when I'm under pressure to change who I am. Give me the strength to walk away from conversations and even from relationships when that's the best thing to do. Teach me how to become more useful to you. I know I can always become a better woman . . . and I want to do that . . . but I don't want to try to change myself to fit someone else's ideas. I only want to please you. That takes a lot of pressure off. Thank you.

Am I now trying to win the approval of human beings, or of God? Or am I trying to please people? If I were still trying to please people, I would not be a servant of Christ.

Galatians 1:10 NIV

60

Beginning and Ending Each Day with Gratitude

Father,

I want to be intentional about beginning and ending each day with gratitude. Your blessings to me are so generous and so constant. I never want to take them for granted. When my eyes flicker open in the morning, before I toss back the covers and my feet hit the floor, I will say thank you that I slept peacefully, secure in the knowledge that you were not asleep but keeping watch over me all night. Thank you for the gift of this new day. I don't know what it holds for me, but you do, and that's all I need to know.

When this day draws to a close and I once again lay my head on my pillow, I will thank you for all that happened in this day—the good and the difficult. I'm grateful for your wisdom that guides my steps and my words. I'm grateful for your protection—even in the times when I didn't know you were protecting me.

Thank you for all you do for me—every day and every night. Your love is obvious . . . and I love you.

The LORD is good and his love endures forever;
  his faithfulness continues through all generations.

  Psalm 100:5 NIV

61

Grateful That You Do Not Condemn Me

Oh God,

My mind is blown by the concept of no condemnation, the truth promised in Romans 8:1–2 that you, the perfect God of all creation, do not condemn me for my rebellion and sin. You just don't. You don't hold it over my head that I continue to sin the same sins that I've asked you to forgive me for over and over. You look at me and see my heart as clean, even though in the next five minutes I'll think, say, or do something selfish. I know that I truly do not deserve this consideration. But I am so thankful that you see me through the filter of Jesus's sacrificial death. That means that you see my sinful, dirty heart as . . . clean! White as snow! This is beyond my understanding. I am humbled. I am grateful. I am blessed. I am beyond condemnation because of Jesus. Thank you for this incredible, undeserved blessing! I don't take it lightly, because each time an unkind thought crosses my mind or a hurtful word spews from my mouth, I am once again grateful that you do not condemn me.

So now there is no condemnation for those who belong to Christ Jesus. And because you belong to him, the power of the life-giving Spirit has freed you from the power of sin that leads to death.

Romans 8:1–2

62

The Honor of Working with God

Father,

It's humbling but kind of cool to realize that you don't *need* me for anything. Your work on earth will get done whether I'm a part of it or not. Your kingdom will endure with or without me. Your plans will continue whether I participate or not. I'm not actually integral to anything you're doing.

It's true that you don't need me; however, you *want* me. How amazing is that? You want me to know you because you love me. You invite me to be a part of your kingdom work because you've gifted me and prepared me to have a role in it. You realize what an incredible privilege it is to serve you, and you want me to experience it, not because you need my work or presence but because you know it will bring joy into my life. You are self-sufficient on your own, so it's an amazing blessing and an incredible honor to be a part of your plan and kingdom work. Thank you for all of this. You give my life meaning and purpose.

You are the light of the world—like a city on a hilltop that cannot be hidden. . . . In the same way, let your good deeds shine out for all to see, so that everyone will praise your heavenly Father.

Matthew 5:14, 16

63

Thank You for Redeeming My Past

Oh my Father,

Who doesn't try to keep their mistakes and bad choices to themselves? I suppose everyone does. I certainly don't want to air my dirty laundry in public. I prefer to walk through it, moment by moment, alone, in the middle of the night. Sigh.

What's done is done, and as much as I want to, I can't change my past. However, I am incredibly grateful to you for redeeming my past by forgiving it, pushing it clear out of your sight, and giving me a positive, hopeful future.

There's another element to the story of my ugly past. You've given me the courage to share about it with some people and the wisdom to know when to do so. It hasn't always been easy. I'm ashamed to admit some of the choices I've made. But I'm grateful that you've encouraged me to tell my story to some who need to hear it. Thank you for using my story to help others so they do not make the same mistakes I did. From my troubled past to today's chances to share with others, nothing is wasted with you, Father, and I appreciate that. Thank you for helping others through hearing my story of how you saved me and lifted me out of the mess.

In him we have redemption through his blood, the forgiveness of our trespasses, according to the riches of his grace.

Ephesians 1:7 ESV

64

God Is Everywhere, Always

Oh Father,

I get myself in some ridiculous dilemmas and situations because of my stubbornness and control issues. Oftentimes I wonder if I've buried myself so deeply that you can't even see what's happening with me, let alone help me out of my mess. Of course, in my heart I know that just isn't true. I love the word *omnipresent* to describe you because it means you are everywhere all the time. And that means I'm never out of your sight. Even when I'm stubborn and rebellious and trying to do things my own way . . . you see me. I can cry out to you for help or protection at three o'clock in the morning or three o'clock in the afternoon . . . and you are there. You never take a day off. You never look away. The problems of little old me are always just as important to you as the massive, horrible problems of the rest of the world. You are big enough, present enough, and powerful enough to handle them all. Thank you for that. Thank you for always being present, for always knowing what's happening, and for always, always loving me.

"Am I a God who is only close at hand?"
        says the LORD.
"No, I am far away at the same time.
Can anyone hide from me in a secret
        place?
Am I not everywhere in all the
        heavens and earth?"
says the LORD.

                    Jeremiah 23:23–24

65

Answers
to Prayer

My loving Father,

Every time I come to you in prayer, I am fully confident that you will answer. That fills my heart with peace and hope. Of course, your answers may not always be exactly what I asked for, and they may not come in the time frame that I would desire. However, I know . . . I believe in my heart . . . that your answers and solutions are best for me and anyone else I've prayed for. The answers I request are often selfish and simple, while your answers lead to faith growth and stronger dependence on you. I confess that I'm sometimes disappointed at first, but I'm working on being submissive and honestly grateful.

Thank you for hearing my prayers. Thank you for wanting me to pray. After all, you actually ask me to tell you what's on my heart. Thank you for answering my prayers always with the most perfect responses. When I see your answer to one prayer, I'm even more motivated to come to you the next time because I know you're listening and acting in your deep love for me. I'm so grateful.

Ask and it will be given to you; seek and you will find; knock and the door will be opened to you.

Matthew 7:7 NIV

66

Awaiting Jesus's Return

Oh Father,

Our world is in such a mess. Watching the evening news or reading about it makes me sad, fearful, and anxious. The horrible things that people in war-torn countries are dealing with; diseases that are out of control; violence played out in grocery stores, schools, and even churches. Natural disasters and poverty and lack of water and food for some parts of the world . . . I could go on and on. But Father, these terrible things bring me to my knees, praying for all the hurting people. And as I pray, I thank you . . . that Jesus is coming back. I know that it's impossible for us to know the day that will happen, but it sure feels like many of the signs you said to look for are happening. I'm grateful to know that he is coming —whenever that may be. Those of us who belong to you will be whisked away from this horror to spend a joyful eternity with you in the beauty of your heaven. Thank you for that promise. Thank you that he's coming. What a beautiful thing to anticipate!

Then, together with them, we who are still alive and remain on the earth will be caught up in the clouds to meet the Lord in the air. Then we will be with the Lord forever.

1 Thessalonians 4:17

67

God's Help
with Grief

Father,

Grief is hard. It's painful. It's constant. There are times when I feel like I can't function because my heart is swallowed by grief. But I've realized something important. I'm grieving now because I was blessed to have loved and been loved. Losing that loved one sent me deep into grief. It wouldn't hurt so much if I hadn't cared so much, and that caring was a gift. So, I want to thank you that I had the blessing of loving someone so much that losing that person fills me with grief.

It's always easy to thank you for the people in my life who love me and whom I love, but when you take them away . . it's difficult and painful to be thankful. I have to take the good with the difficult. I miss my loved one a lot, and I always will. I'm thankful for the time we had together, the fun we had, the experiences we shared, and the memories we made. Those memories will sustain me now. Thank you for love. Thank you for grief. Thank you for your presence and strength to help me through grieving.

---

*If your heart is broken, you'll find GOD right there;
if you're kicked in the gut, he'll help you catch your breath.*

Psalm 34:18 The Message

68

God Is Light

Father,

I am so grateful for your light. Thank you that there is no darkness in you at all, only life-giving, darkness-filling light. When I lose my way in the darkness, when I can't see if there is a solid place to put my foot down, when I can only imagine the monsters hiding in the darkness, I have only to cry out to you.

Your light may be just a tiny pinprick far away in the murky darkness, but it gives me a direction to lock my eyes on. Or your light may be a brilliance that fills every corner so that all darkness is immediately blasted away. No matter how it comes, I'm incredibly thankful for your brilliant, incredible, life-saving light. What a relief to look into total darkness and see even a tiny light. It means I'm not alone. It gives me peace that you're there, guiding and directing, and as long as I keep my eyes, heart, and mind glued to the light, I can move forward out of the darkness. Your light means hope. Thank you for it.

Once again Jesus spoke to the people. This time he said, "I am the light for the world! Follow me, and you won't be walking in the dark. You will have the light that gives life."

John 8:12 CEV

69

God's Gracious, Blessed Mercy

Oh Lord,

Thank you for the precious gift of your mercy. I humbly admit that you have every reason and every right to punish me firmly, endlessly, and righteously, but because of your mercy, you don't. You could certainly give up on me because of my disobedience and my habit of repeating the same old sins, but you don't. You could simply cut me off and never pay any attention to me again, but you don't.

Mercy means you are constantly kind, and even when you are disciplining me, I am aware of your love. Mercy means you are compassionate—hurting because I hurt, caring about my pain, and helping me through the difficult times. Sometimes your compassionate help is so obvious; sometimes it's below the surface and I don't even recognize it until I look back later. Thank you for your mercy. It's truly undeserved, but I'm so very grateful for it.

It is God who decides to show mercy. We can neither choose it nor work for it.

Romans 9:16

70

God's Knowledge of the Future

My loving God,

I'm so very thankful that you can see into the future. Your Word tells me that you began making plans for my life even before I was born. Nothing that happens to me surprises you, and wow, that is the most peace-giving, confidence-securing thought ever. Even when I was a child, you were already preparing me for things I'd face as an adult, for work that I'd do and relationships I'd have. I'm often reminded that you planted that sycamore tree decades before

Zacchaeus needed to climb it. How wonderful that you see the past, the present, and what's ahead for me, well . . . for all of us. Since you do know what's coming, you prepare me for it, even though I don't realize that's what you're doing. I'm so grateful.

With your own eyes you saw
my body being formed.
Even before I was born,
you had written in your book
everything about me.

Psalm 139:16 CEV

71

Thankful I Can Share My Faith with Others

Father,

Thank you for the incredible privilege to be able to share my faith with others. I am especially grateful for the times when the topic comes up organically and I can simply explain how asking Jesus into my heart has given my life meaning and purpose. I'm pleased that I can share how your love brings peace, security, and guidance into my life. I'm happy to be able to dispel any preconceived notions of how becoming a Christ-follower imprisons rather than frees me.

What joy you bring into my life, Father. I want others to know that joy, and I know that you want them to know it also. I love that I can share your grace, mercy, and forgiveness too. I'm grateful that I can tell others about what a comfort it is to be able to pray and about how I see your answers all the time. I'm happy to share how reading your Word gives me great peace and comfort. Thank you for trusting me with this responsibility and privilege and for giving me the best words to speak as I share.

But in your hearts revere Christ as Lord. Always be prepared to give an answer to everyone who asks you to give the reason for the hope that you have.

1 Peter 3:15 NIV

72

Thank You for the Sacrifices of Missionaries

My gracious Lord,

I am humbled by the people you have called to leave their homes and families behind and move to other parts of the world to tell people about you. These missionaries are fulfilling your call to go to the "ends of the earth" to make sure all people have the opportunity to hear about your love. Thank you for all who have answered that call. It must be hard sometimes to be in a different culture, to miss family back home, and to sometimes face opposition to your message.

Thank you for the privilege I have of praying for the missionaries: for the relationships they build and the opportunities for them to witness to people. I pray for their safety and their well-being, physically, emotionally, and spiritually. Thank you that I can support them financially as they do your work in other parts of the world. I appreciate having a part in their ministry.

Your Word tells me that you want all people to have the opportunity to know Jesus. I'm grateful that I can share about you here at home and that I can pray for and give to that work around the world.

But you will receive power when the Holy Spirit comes upon you. And you will be my witnesses, telling people about me everywhere—in Jerusalem, throughout Judea, in Samaria, and to the ends of the earth.

Acts 1:8

73

Places of Peace

Dear Father,

We all need places where we can just *be* and let your loving Spirit flow through our souls, washing away the stress and tensions of these times. Thank you for the many places you've created where we can settle into your soul-cleansing peace. For me, it's anywhere near water, whether on the shore of a peaceful lake, on the bank of a river, or sitting by the ocean. In any of these places, I sense the stress fade away from my body. I feel my soul take a deep breath and exhale away anxiety, frustration, and other peace-stealing emotions I've been harboring.

Thank you for this simple refuge. I'm filled with gratitude that you have created so many beautiful places for us. I know some folks find their peaceful spots in the mountains, some prefer meadows or fields. Some like the ocean. But Lord, in your great love and wisdom, you made a place for each of us to be able to step out of our busy, chaotic lives and just . . . *be*. You knew we'd need places like these to refuel. Thank you for each one. Thank you that in our refuges, your Spirit meets us, speaking to us, calming our hearts, and loving us so tenderly.

In the beginning God created the heavens and the earth.

Genesis 1:1

74

Lessons through Illness

Dear Father,

I'm sick. I mean I feel really crummy. I've been in bed for several days and it's making me crazy. I'm used to being busy and on the run. It's hard to be still because even though I'm not feeling well, I want to get up and do things!

I never thought I'd do this, but . . . I want to thank you for this illness. Yes, it's taken me a few days to realize this, but I'm beginning to see why it's good for me to be flat on my back right now. You've slowed me down. I've had time to think about a lot of things over the last few days. Things like how I've been treating others, or if my priorities have gotten skewed, or if I've made other things more important in my schedule than spending time with you. Thank you for giving me time to evaluate where my life is headed. Thank you for helping me see that I need to depend on you, for health, for strength, for keeping life on track. I probably wouldn't have realized some of these things if my busy life were still so busy. Thank you for speaking with me in the quietness of the night. Thank you for gentle challenges. Thank you for helping me rewind and restart . . . on a better path.

> *Steep your life in God-reality, God-initiative, God-provisions. Don't worry about missing out. You'll find all your everyday human concerns will be met.*
>
> Matthew 6:33 *The Message*

75

I'm Glad You Are a Jealous God

Father,

I know this is going to sound weird, but I want to thank you that you are a jealous God. Strange thing to be thankful for, right? You've shared stories in the Bible about people who tried to worship you *and* something else, and it never went well for them.

Sometimes I'm tempted to add an *and* to my worship—a person, money, success—whatever it might be. When I remember that your Word says you are a jealous God who will not share my worship, that pulls me back to reality.

So, thank you that you want *all* of me. I don't want to try to put anything on the same level as you in my heart because you deserve all of me, and I want you to have all my honor, worship, respect, and obedience. You are number one in my heart, and I'm grateful for that.

You must worship no other gods, for the Lord, whose very name is Jealous, is a God who is jealous about his relationship with you.

Exodus 34:14

76

God Is Still Working!

Father,

You are still working! Thank you! You're still changing hearts. You're still guiding people. You're still in control of everything. I feel deep peace because I know you are still working. I'm grateful that even though people in our world have become so much like the people of Noah's day, you haven't wiped us all out. You haven't given up! You are working on us, one person at a time . . . and I'm one of those.

Sometimes when horrific things happen in our world or in my life, I may ask if you noticed or why you didn't prevent it. But the bottom line is that I trust that you have your reasons and that the people who were hurt or who lost loved ones or homes sense your presence and your provision. I trust that your people (including me) will step up to help as you speak to our hearts and motivate us to get busy. Thank you, Father, that you're still working.

I will give them an undivided heart and put a new spirit in them, I will remove from them their heart of stone and give them a heart of flesh.

Ezekiel 11:19 NIV

77

Gratitude for New Life

Gracious Father,

I am simply blown away by the miracle of birth. I mean . . . I'm speechless. This tiny human being I'm holding in my arms is evidence of your love, your wisdom and knowledge, and your power and creativity. Thank you for her. Thank you that I have the privilege to be a part of her life. Thank you for the honor of being a member of the "village" that plays with her, laughs with her, sings with her, and reads with her. Thank you for allowing me to have a role in teaching her about you and for the true privilege of intentionally praying for her every day. Thank you that there are many people, both family and friends, who will feed into this little girl so that she knows she is deeply loved and treasured.

I do pray, Father, that she comes to know you early so she can spend her lifetime learning about you and basking in your love and care. Keep her safe. Protect her from any who would seek to harm her. And Father, help me be a positive, encouraging, loving mentor to her. Thank you for this precious new life.

Don't you see that children are GOD's best gift?
the fruit of the womb his generous legacy?

Psalm 127:3 The Message

78

Blessedness of Faith's Reward

Father,

One of my favorite stories in the Bible is about the woman who had been sick for twelve years—not only sick but unclean because of her sickness. I'm grateful for the story of her courage. Oh, what incredible courage she must have had to squeeze through the crowd so she could reach Jesus. And her faith—oh Lord, I want faith like that. She believed that just touching his robe could heal her. I love that Jesus rewarded her faith by healing her.

Thank you, Father, for this story. It encourages me that you see my faith and my desire for it to grow stronger, and you reward that hope. Thank you for Jesus's loving words that ended twelve years of struggle for that woman. His words cleansed her, allowing her to return to society. Thank you that she didn't give up. I'm grateful that you knew what an encouragement and blessing this story would be to me and to many others, I'm sure. It encourages my heart.

Don't be afraid, for I am with you.
Don't be discouraged, for I am your
God.
I will strengthen you and help you.
I will hold you up with my victorious
right hand.

Isaiah 41:10

79

Thankfulness in the Good Times

My dear Father,

Everything in my life is going well right now. I'm sorry to say that it's often during these times when I neglect to thank you for this much-needed oasis of peace and tranquility. Thank you that my family relationships are filled with love and happiness. Thank you that my friendships are peaceful, encouraging, and supportive. Thank you that I enjoy my job, that my superiors are encouraging, and that the work is mentally challenging and interesting. Thank you that (for the time being) I'm not consumed with anxiety about life. Of course, I know you are always in control, so there's no reason for anxiety, but . . . you know.

I just want to thank you for everything right now, while life is good—in fact, *because* life is good. I'm not asking for anything. I'm not worried about anything. Thank you for all you do for me, day in and day out. Thank you for times of peace. Thank you that I know I can trust you for all things, in good times and difficult times.

Our Lord and Ruler,
your name is wonderful
everywhere on earth!
You let your glory be seen
in the heavens above.

Psalm 8:1 CEV

80

Praying for One Another

Dear Father,

Thank you for those dear ones who have prayed for me through the years. I know there have been many. Thank you for my grandmothers, who loved and honored you and began praying for me before I was even born. They wanted me to know you and to come to faith early in my life. Thank you for the ones who picked up that gauntlet after my grandmothers were gone. My own parents. Friends who mentored me in my teen years. My spiritual mother. Even my peers—same age as me but older in their faith. And now, equals, friends, coworkers, family. We're all in the faith journey together. We support each other and lift each other up to you.

The prayers of all these people have helped mold me into the woman I am today. I wouldn't be here if it weren't for them. Thank you for their faithful prayers. They pray because they care and because they know their prayers make a difference. I'm so very grateful for them and that you always have someone to fill that role in my life. Thank you.

Keep on asking, and you will receive what you ask for. Keep on seeking, and you will find. Keep on knocking, and the door will be opened to you.

Luke 11:9

81

Praise You for Your Holiness

My Father,

I am amazed, humbled, and grateful for your holiness. Your holiness reflects your majesty and your purity. Holiness sets you apart from any other being. Your goodness means you are not capable of evil. You are always fair and honest. Your love is wrapped in holiness, so when you look at me, your heart is filled with warmth toward me. You want the best for me, and you will never compromise when it comes to your own standards or your wishes for me. It's all beyond my comprehension. You are always present, always wise, and always working.

All these parts of your holiness draw me to you. I long to know you and to be close to you. Thank you for your holiness that makes you far above me, holiness that is unattainable for me. Still you love me and want to be close to me. In your holiness, you want to teach me, grow me, protect me, and love me.

Holy, holy, holy is the Lord God, the Almighty—
the one who always was, who is, and who is still to come.

Revelation 4:8

82

Thank You
for Endings

Dear Father,

Honestly, this is hard to say, but I know I must:
Thank you for endings. Yes, I mean it . . . or
at least I want to mean it. Endings are painful,
especially when I don't want the end to come.
When a precious relationship ends, it leaves a
painful wound in the heart. There's confusion
and hurt. When a loved one dies, the emptiness
is sometimes unbearable. When a job ends but
not by my own choice, there's embarrassment,
fear, confusion, and sadness.

Endings come in many ways, but they generally aren't welcome. And yet I am learning that, oftentimes, without endings there couldn't be beginnings. Saying goodbye to people and things I care about is difficult and painful, but I see how it is sometimes necessary for you to cull things from my life—things that may not be the best. This is also a way to open my time, my life, and my interests to new things. So, thank you for endings, as hard as they are, and thank you for the beginnings that follow those endings.

We may make a lot of plans,
but the LORD will do
what he has decided.
Proverbs 19:21 CEV

83

You Keep Your Promises

Heavenly Father,

I've learned—sometimes the hard way—that people cannot always be trusted to keep their promises. When they promise something without thinking or on the spur of the moment or in a moment of passion, it may turn out that the promise cannot be kept. But what's really hard is when those people attempt to lie their way out of the broken promise.

These experiences make me even more grateful that you, Father, always keep your promises. Always. I can read through your Word and highlight every promise you make to any who choose to follow you. There are thousands of promises, and that's a lot to keep track of. However, you remember each of them, and you keep each of them. Always. You do not make excuses or try to justify why you can't keep your promises. What a joyful comfort that is, Father. Thank you that I can always trust you. Thank you that you do not lie—cannot lie—because it would go against your character. Thank you for all of that, Father. These truths make my faith grow stronger and stronger.

Because of his glory and excellence, he has given us great and precious promises. These are the promises that enable you to share his divine nature and escape the world's corruption caused by human desires.

2 Peter 1:4

84

Thank You for Giving Me Time

Father,

You know that I've been in a bad place for a while. Over and over again I've asked you to change the pressures of certain situations I'm facing. I've even asked you to change other people's opinions, attitudes, and . . . yes, even their hearts because I want everything to be the way I want it. I humbly confess my impatience and sometimes even feelings of hopelessness that you even hear my prayers, let alone that you will answer them.

But today I realized something incredible: Over the last few weeks, there *have* been changes. But the changes weren't in the situations or any of the people . . . they were in me. Today I was humming a happy tune when it suddenly hit me that I'm not feeling as negative or hopeless as I was before. Improving my attitude and my trust in you is certainly still a work in progress, but it is happening. Thank you for giving me time to adjust, even though it is a struggle. Thank you that I'm beginning to see some good in what I'm learning, and that leads to my starting to believe again that you do hear my prayers and you will answer, in your own time and in your own way. And . . . it's all good.

Wait for the Lord;
be strong and take heart
and wait for the Lord.

Psalm 27:14 NIV

85

The Beauty of Surprises

Father,

Thank you for surprises. I love it when I'm going along in my day and something unexpected but really pleasant happens . . . and I know it comes from you. It must give you pleasure to drop those little sunbursts of joy into our lives. It's always unexpected. It may not be a huge thing, but something like bumping into a dear friend just when I need a hug or seeing a cardinal perched on my fence, or once or twice it's been a fit of soul-filling laughter with a child. Wow, that's fun! Some people call these moments "God winks"—evidence of your presence with us every moment. Evidence of your delight in dropping moments of unexpected joy into our lives. Thank you that these God winks often come at a time when I really need a pick-me-up, a reminder of your love. Thank you for the moments when I look to the heavens and whisper, "I know that was you. Thank you." Being able to do that brings me great joy!

Every good gift and every perfect gift is from above, coming down from the Father of lights, with whom there is no variation or shadow due to change.

James 1:17 ESV

86

Thankful
I Am Right
Where I Am

Gracious God,

Thank you that you have put me in this place at this moment in time. I know my presence here is your idea and your plan. I've struggled with being in this physical place because of the changes it has meant in my work and relationships. Even though I don't always see what my purpose is or why I am where I am, I believe and trust that you are controlling those details. I'm grateful that you have a plan for my life, and I trust your plan, even when I can't see the good in it at the moment.

I want to be useful to you. I want to be obedient to you. I want to be intentional about doing whatever work you put in my path. I'm grateful for the life you've given me. I'm sorry for the times I've complained about things in my life. I'm sorry for the time I have wasted being bored or just plain-old negative.

Father, I realize that life is indeed a gift. Serving you is a privilege. Being even a tiny part of your kingdom work is an honor. Thank you, God, that I am *here*.

We know that God causes everything to work together for the good of those who love God and are called according to his purpose for them.

Romans 8:28

87

Thank You for Victory!

Dear Lord,

Sometimes I just feel defeated. No real reason. I know I give in to sin too often. I let Satan get a foothold in my heart, and I don't know how to kick him out. Then I'm disappointed in myself, and I feel like you must be disappointed in me as well. When I feel that way, Satan wins.

But wait—no, he doesn't!

Oh God, I am so very grateful that because Jesus is in my heart, I have victory. I have victory! I need to say it again—I have victory!

Satan cannot win because I will keep coming to you, asking for your help, listening for the Holy Spirit's guidance, and grabbing on to your strength. And you will give me victory by pushing Satan away. Your love is never more evident than when you lift me out of the pit that the Evil One has buried me in. I'm grateful that you're always with me, watching out for me, loving me, and waiting for my cry for help when I've had enough of my own choices. Thank you, dear God, for victory that comes only through you and by you!

But thank God! He gives us victory over sin and death through our Lord Jesus Christ.

1 Corinthians 15:57

88

Freedom in Christ

Father God,

Some people say that becoming a Christian is like becoming a slave. They say that when I asked Christ into my life, it was suddenly not my own anymore because you are my Master and now dictate everything I do or say and how I spend my time. That's hogwash. I have more freedom now than I've ever had.

Thank you for freedom from the anxiety of being punished for my sins, since Christ himself took on my punishment. Thank you that

I'm free to be the person you made me to be. Staying close to you and studying your Word keeps me strong against Satan's temptation so I escape being caught in his web of deceit. I have freedom to say, "Get out of here, Satan. Help me, Jesus!" I know that your strength and power are immediately mine, and because of that, Satan runs away. Thank you for the freedom of absolutely knowing that my eternity with you in heaven is secure. Nothing can change that. Freedom to be me. Freedom to know my future is secure. Freedom to do what you've gifted me to do. Thank you for my freedom.

Christ has set us free to live a free life. So take your stand! Never again let anyone put a harness of slavery on you.

Galatians 5:1 The Message

89

Thank You for My Family

Father,

I'm thankful for the family you gave me. I know there are people who don't have a loving, supportive family. I'm sorry for those people. I pray that you will guide them. That makes me even more thankful for the experiences I had growing up. I appreciate my dad's sense of humor. He could make me laugh till tears rolled down my cheeks. I loved how very hard he and my mom worked to provide for our family, yet they made time to come to my sports events and concerts. Thank you that they listened to me tell stories and ask questions—even when they were tired.

Thank you for parents who were serious about their faith. They loved you and encouraged me to come to know you early. Thank you for their prayers for me and for the examples they were as people on the journey to know Christ deeply. They took me to Sunday school and to church. They showed me that it matters to have a faith family. They helped me become the woman I am today. Thank you for them.

And give thanks for everything to God the Father in the name of our Lord Jesus Christ.

Ephesians 5:20

90

Heavenly Reminders

My Father,

Some days I get so caught up in . . . me. My focus turns inward, and I see only my short-comings and failures. My thoughts become negative and self-condemning. I become un-able (or unwilling) to recognize or empathize with anyone else's pain or problems. Life is simply all about me, and I want your attention to be fully, completely, only . . . on me.

But then my eyes slowly open to things like the vastness of the night sky with a bazillion twinkling stars, and I remember the world is a lot bigger than just me. Thank you for reminding me of that. Thank you for my happy place when I'm sitting by the ocean, watching the waves crash onto the shore. I look out and see nothing but ocean, and I remember once again that the world is a lot bigger than just me. Thank you for reminders that there are thousands of people in this world, and many, or even most of them, have tougher issues to deal with than I do. I am grateful that you gently get me out of my own head and help me realize that the world is bigger than my experiences. It puts things in perspective and opens my mind to your greatness, love, and care.

If I could speak all the languages of earth and of angels, but didn't love others, I would only be a noisy gong or a clanging cymbal.

1 Corinthians 13:1

91

You Are God
and I Am Not

God,

What a mess our world is. It's heartbreaking
and terrifying, and then heartbreaking again.
Oh God, what are we doing? I mean, really, what
are we doing to each other and to this planet?
Daily I think about how very grateful I am that
you are God and I am not. But then I wonder
how badly your heart must hurt because of the
wars in which innocent people are murdered,
including children, God—children! Some of
these "wars" aren't military battles but gangs

on city streets or people walking into schools or churches or grocery stores and gunning down people they don't even know. The hatred. The disregard for human life. I'm heartbroken.

Father, I'm relieved that dealing with the violence and hatred in our world is not on my shoulders—except to be intentional and certain that I don't contribute to it. I'm responsible for my choices, attitudes, behaviors, and obedience to you. I'm eternally grateful that I am not God—you are. You know what's happening here. You're working even though some of us aren't responding. You care. I know, Father, that you care. Show us how to have a part in stopping the violence, hatred, and killing.

Trust in the LORD forever,
  for the LORD, the LORD himself, is the Rock eternal.

Isaiah 26:4 NIV

92

Your Powerful Love

Oh Father,

Sometimes I'm so blatantly critical of you, your work, your people. Thank you for still loving me. I'm often judgmental of other Christians and how they live their lives. Thank you for still loving me. I have a tendency to be critical of anyone who is different from me without even knowing them personally. Thank you for still loving me. Sometimes I'm lazy about praying for others. Thank you for still loving me.

Sometimes I'm lazy about spending time in your Word. Thank you for still loving me.

You put up with all my shortcomings—my complaints, my criticisms, my failures—and you just keep loving me. Thank you that nothing can separate me from your love. It's so strong, so complete, and the only thing you ever ask from me is the obedience to your tenets that grows from my love for you. I love you, Father. I love you.

For I am convinced that neither death nor life, neither angels nor demons, neither the present nor the future, nor any powers, neither height nor depth, nor anything else in all creation, will be able to separate us from the love of God that is in Christ Jesus our Lord.

Romans 8:38–39 NIV

93

You Are
the Only Truth

Father,

Something scaring me in our culture today is
that there doesn't seem to be absolute truth. I
feel like we've become so politically correct in
being tolerant of others' beliefs and opinions
that we've pushed aside what is actually true.
Some of us try to be accepting, and some of
us become belligerent and pharisaical in our
opinions and attitudes.

Oh God, thank you that truth is found in
you. Only in you. Thank you that the words

of Scripture are true—not what I wish they said, but what they actually say is true. Always true. Thank you that when we stand for your truth, no one loses. Thank you that when we follow your teaching and take a stand for truth, clothed in love and grace, all of us can win. Your truth wins. It's not always easy, but by your power we can stand for truth. Strengthen me. Show me how. Remind me to wear the cloak of respect, kindness, and grace as I stand for your truth.

We will speak the truth in love, growing in every way more and more like Christ, who is the head of his body, the church.

Ephesians 4:15

94

I Am Holy!

Precious Father,

Every day you change me. Each time I read your Word, I learn how you desire for me to live, how to be more like Jesus. Every moment I spend talking with you, I feel your Spirit grow stronger in my heart. Each time I face my own sins and confess them to you, I sense a strong urge to repent . . . to turn away from those behaviors. You *are* changing me. I never dreamed that I could be holy. But I can . . . though, for sure, I am a work in progress.

Thank you for teaching me about Christ's character and for growing that character in me.

I know I'm not always an A+ student, but you never give up on me. You look at my heart, my desires, and my yearnings, and you see what I can be! Thank you for that. You see that I sometimes take a step or two forward, then fall back, but I learn from each failure. You already see me as holy because you see me through the filter of Jesus's love, sacrifice, and victory. Thank you. Praise you, and thank you again!

For the Scriptures say, "You must be holy because I am holy."

1 Peter 1:16

95

Thank You for Reining Me In

Father,

Thank you for reining me in. Wow, do I ever need your Spirit to pull me back, shut my mouth, and control my facial expressions and eye rolls. Thank you for doing all that for me, in an instant, before I've hurt or offended someone. I think it's partly a result of our social media–infused culture that my opinions have become so . . . opinionated. Like many others, I sometimes freely share unsolicited ideas and thoughts—not always kindly. Even though I really try to form my opinions and beliefs based on your Word, sometimes they become colored by my feelings or those of people I read, follow, or listen to. (They aren't always right.)

Thank you for pulling me back from spouting words I don't need to share. Thank you for shutting my mouth when the words were going to come out unkindly and disrespectfully. Thank you for keeping my face from showing what I'm thinking. Thank you for stopping those irritating eye rolls. Thank you for reminding me that I need to love my neighbor as myself . . . even if we disagree.

"The most important commandment is this: 'Listen, O Israel! The LORD our God is the one and only LORD. And you must love the LORD your God with all your heart, all your soul, all your mind, and all your strength." The second is equally important: "Love your neighbor as yourself." No other commandment is greater than these.

Mark 12:29–31

96

Your Work in Me

My loving heavenly Father,

I can't even find the words to thank you for your deep, unconditional love for me. It's more than I can conceive. It's more than I deserve. It's more than I understand. You never stop loving me. You want such amazing things for me. Your plan is for me to have a wonderful life, filled with the joy of knowing you and the fulfillment of serving you. Thank you for working hard to make that happen by loving me and drawing me to you. Thank you for never tiring of working in my heart, teaching me, and challenging me. Thank you for your endless energy and boundless strength! You give me so much. You love me so well. I am grateful to you!

I ask—ask the God of our Master, Jesus Christ, the God of glory—to make you intelligent and discerning in knowing him personally, your eyes focused and clear, so that you can see exactly what it is he is calling you to do, grasp the immensity of this glorious way of life he has for his followers, oh, the utter extravagance of his work in us who trust him—endless energy, boundless strength!

Ephesians 1:19 The Message

97

Thanks
for the Secret

Father,

Thank you for the truth found in Colossians 3:3. I'm thankful because this simple verse tells me how to discover my life in you. I need only to learn how Jesus lived when he was on this earth. After all, my ultimate goal is to be like him and to love as he did. I'm grateful for your Word in which I can learn what Jesus taught. I can read his very words. I can see how he interacted with people. I recognize his love for common folks who were struggling to know how to do the right things. I see his disdain for the actions of the religious leaders who perverted your Word. I see his compassion for all who were hurting. I see his desire for all people to know your love. Jesus lived what he taught were the two most important commandments—to love God with all our heart, soul, mind, and strength and to love our neighbor as ourself (Mark 12:30–31). I know you want me to live those out loud in my life too. Thank you for sharing what Jesus's words, care, and love looked like while he was a man walking this earth. Help me to learn and to live as he did.

For you died to this life, and your real life is hidden with Christ in God.

Colossians 3:3

98

Thankful for the Lord's Prayer

Father,

My prayers can so easily become a list of "God, do this," as though I dare to instruct you about how you run this world and especially about how you handle my life. I'm sorry for that. I'm grateful that Jesus gave a diagram of how to pray by sharing what has become known as the Lord's Prayer. Teach me through it, Father, as I recognize your position as my Father in heaven and praise your hallowed name. Humble me to submit to your kingdom and your will on earth as it is in heaven. Remind me to pray for my simple needs this day, not my wants, and to ask your forgiveness for my shortcomings, and also to forgive any who hurt me. Thank you for the reminder that if I obey you, I won't fall to temptation but will be protected by your Spirit. Oh God, I praise you that yours is the kingdom, power, and glory forever! Thank you for Jesus's simple, beautiful, humble prayer . . . a diagram of how to speak to you.

Jesus said, "This is how you should pray:

"Father, may your name be kept holy.
    May your Kingdom come soon.
Give us each day the food we need,
and forgive us our sins,
    as we forgive those who sin against us.
And don't let us yield to temptation."

Luke 11:2–4

99

Thank You for Taking Away My Guilt

Father,

It's often about three a.m. when the guilt monster arrives. He taps me on my shoulder, waking me from my sound sleep, and begins the lengthy video of my lifetime of failures. He really punches home the times I've hurt people—intentionally or unknowingly. He convinces me that you are disgusted with me and really have no use for me. That's the end of sleep for that night. Guilt consumes me. Tears flow. Things I can't change become the definition of my life.

Then your gentle Spirit whispers into my heart. Oh Father, I'm grateful—forever grateful—for the whisper that reminds me that the guilt monster is lying. Yes, my failures are real. Yes, I've hurt people. But never have you been disgusted with me. Never have you given up on me. Guilt is a lie. Thank you for that truth. Thank you for forgiveness and grace. Thank you for fresh starts. Thank you for your love.

But if we confess our sins to him, he is faithful and just to forgive us our sins and to cleanse us from all wickedness.

1 John 1:9

100

Praise, Gratitude, and Thankfulness

Father,

I am not going to ask you for anything right now. I just worship you for who you are. I'm grateful to be your daughter. Your love for me is rich and pure every moment. Your presence in my life is a blessing of protection, guidance, and purpose. The gentleness of your hand in my life shows me the tenderness of your love.

I praise you for your creation. So much of nature brings me peace and joy and leads me to worship and praise. The vastness of the universe shows me the majesty of who you are.

I'm filled with gratitude and worship for Jesus coming to earth. Thank you for his loving sacrifice. Oh God, I can worship you because of his coming . . . his willingness to suffer and die . . . because of his love.

I worship you, my great and loving Father. You are all I want and all I need. I praise you for today and for the promise of eternity with you!

Honor the wonderful name
of the LORD,
and worship the LORD
most holy and glorious.

Psalm 29:2 CEV

Index of Prayers by Topic

Carolyn Larsen is the bestselling author of more than fifty books for children and adults. She has been a speaker for women's events and classes around the world, bringing scriptural messages filled with humor and tenderness. For more information, visit carolynlarsen.com and follow her on Facebook @CarolynLarsen.